THE CAMBRIDGE TO KING'S LYNN LINE: 30 YEARS OF ELECTRIFICATION

MIKE BECKETT

AMBERLEY

THE CAMBRIDGE TO KING'S LYNN LINE SIMPLIFIED DIAGRAM

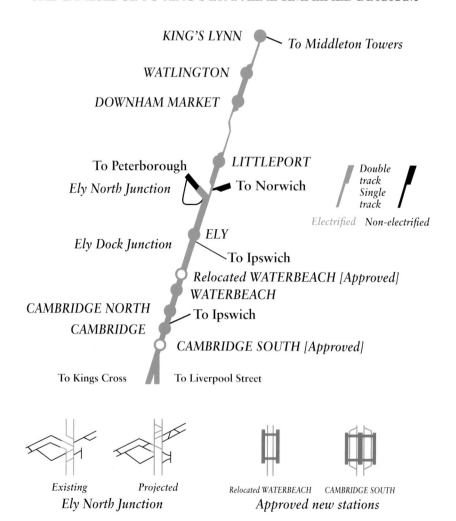

Ely North Junction

Existing   Projected

Ely North Junction

Relocated WATERBEACH   CAMBRIDGE SOUTH

Approved new stations

First published 2023

Amberley Publishing
The Hill, Stroud
Gloucestershire, GL5 4EP

www.amberley-books.com

Copyright © Mike Beckett, 2023

The right of Mike Beckett to be identified as
the Author of this work has been asserted in
accordance with the Copyrights, Designs and
Patents Act 1988.

ISBN 978 1 3981 1558 3 (print)
ISBN 978 1 3981 1559 0 (ebook)

British Library Cataloguing in Publication Data.
A catalogue record for this book is available from
the British Library.

Origination by Amberley Publishing.
Printed in the UK.

Introduction

Winter 1984/5 – the future for the Cambridge–King's Lynn 'Fen Line' looked bleak. BR had singled the 10-mile Littleport–Downham Market section from 17 June 1984. From 14 October, between Magdalen Road (now Watlington) and Kings Lynn Junction (5 miles), only the Down (northbound) line was in use until, on 10 February 1985, the former Up (London-bound) road became a permanent Up and Down single line. True, singling 4 miles between Ely North Junction and Littleport (envisaged in February 1983's 'One Way Ahead?' proposals) wouldn't happen, but, given government attitudes and recent history, even that wasn't certain.

Let's go back to the start. Cambridge–Ely was part of a double-track London–Norwich route, opening on 30 July 1845. Constructed in stages, Lynn–Ely joined it on 25 October 1847. There were single lines between Watlington and Downham, and between Hilgay Fen and Ely North Junction, these being progressively doubled between 1881 and 1884. Then, 100 years later, single lines had come back.

Two decades before the winter of 1984/5, Beeching had recommended retention of Cambridge–Lynn. That was in 1963, coincidentally when the DP3 project – rebuilding 'Baby Deltic' D5901 for Liverpool Street–Lynn – was abandoned. Then, come 1965, Beeching suggested that in East Anglia only the East Coast Main Line (ECML) and the London–Norwich route (via Ipswich, not Cambridge) had a firm future. Internal railway maps that year projected Ely–Lynn as just a freight feeder, branching from the Peterborough–Ipswich route, and that Cambridge–Ely would close entirely within fifteen years.

Politics intervened, and the following year the entire Cambridge–Lynn route was designated 'long term'. However, in 1967 it became apparent that services could be changed or withdrawn anyway. Singling was seen as another 'modernisation' and a scheme to single Littleport–Lynn was prepared the next year. Then everything was thrown into doubt, when the 'Rail Policy Review' was leaked in October 1972 – no railway at all northwards from Cambridge. The government said 'no decisions taken'. But eventually one was, and was fully implemented by February 1985. Singling.

Signalling renewals, meanwhile, had helped justify electrification outwards from London. Liverpool Street–Stortford electrics had run since 1960. Eighteen years later, on 8 May 1978, Kings Cross–Hitchin–Royston went electric and Kings Cross–Cambridge 'Buffet Expresses' ceased. Stock was redeployed to Liverpool Street–Cambridge, filling gaps between two-hourly Lynn services. From 14 May 1979, in response to the new M11, several off-peak Lynn services started running nonstop south of Cambridge – diesel traction, of course.

'Anglia West' electrification (Stortford–Cambridge and Royston–Cambridge), with 'Anglia East' to follow, was proposed in 1980. Get Royston wired and reroute trains to Kings Cross, so the West Anglia Main Line (WAML) could cope with disruption. The next year, government prioritised 'Anglia East'!

Serpell's 1983 report confirmed the value of the ECML and London–Norwich via Ipswich. He saw Liverpool Street–Cambridge as a commuter route – everything else in Cambridgeshire and Norfolk was suspect. Any Cambridge–Lynn survival would depend on subsidy levels. Politics erupted again and negative talk quietened. Indeed, by dropping the proposed EMU depot at Cambridge and using newly released maintenance capacity at Ilford, the Stortford route got its electrification go-ahead in 1984. Later that year, ECML electrification from Hitchin to Edinburgh, including an electrification depot at Peterborough, was also given the green light. All this seemed a great contrast to the Cambridge–Lynn situation during that bleak 1984/5 winter.

Yet, by exploiting that nearby Peterborough depot, in summer 1985 BR was reckoning seven electric locos with push-pull driving trailers could replace six electrics and four diesels if wires reached Lynn. The projected Stansted Airport branch's electrical feeder station would assist. More singling north of Ely, along with a 500-metre holding loop north of Ely North Junction and 300-metre loops at Littleport, Downham and Magdalen Road, would too.

Network SouthEast (NSE) was formed on 10 June 1986 – who will ever forget a £3 Network Day? That year saw the Stansted branch approved. On 4 March 1987 Royston–Cambridge wiring was authorised on a 'smallest loss' basis. On 23 March, the first Liverpool Street–Cambridge electric train (a special) brought the Transport Minister to Cambridge to flag off the first Royston works train. On the front of that train was 47576 *King's Lynn*. No coincidence!

From 11 May, through trains changed locos at Cambridge. Electric 86s handed over to diesel 47s for the Lynn leg. Inefficient, resource-demanding, almost life-expired stock – the solution, electrification? My then employer, the Borough Council of King's Lynn & West Norfolk, received a mildly encouraging draft appraisal that year – modest financial improvements if electrified to Lynn. However, the best-performing options were 'Express Sprinter' 158s on existing or hourly frequencies. Still through trains to London, but *not* electrics.

The formal investment appraisal of 16 February 1988 disappointed. Apart from the status quo (renewals when necessary), there were seventeen options. Six required no new electrification: through 321s with diesel push-pull, Cambridge–Lynn; London–Lynn 158s (existing and hourly frequencies); two-car Leyland 'Sprinter' 155s connecting with Class 321 EMUs at Cambridge on existing frequency; and Provincial sector Cambridge–Ely DMUs connecting at Cambridge with Class 86s and/or 321s, both these with buses onwards to Lynn.

Electrification to Ely only (seven options) entailed: electric/diesel loco swaps at Ely with extra peak 321s; London–Lynn 158s, plus extra 321s to Ely; and splitting the service at Ely. Splitting included permutations of 86s and/or 321s on existing/hourly frequencies with 155s to Lynn; and 321s to Ely with buses beyond. The four 'wires to Lynn' options tested 86s or 321s throughout, on existing and hourly frequencies.

Overall, nine options would keep through London–Lynn trains. One meant changing at Cambridge, five at Ely, two at both. Three meant Ely–Lynn buses. Direct costs and revenues were quantified, as were savings gained from using that Peterborough depot, and external revenue support possibilities were mentioned.

Eight of these options were tested further with an 'advanced' timescale using the Peterborough depot. The two best 'advanced' options required wires to Ely and 'Sprinter' 155 shuttles from Ely to Lynn, either on existing frequency or hourly, in that order of preference. With a standalone project, not using Peterborough depot, a Cambridge–Lynn 155 shuttle performed best.

From April, Anglia Region (split from Eastern) was created, working closely with NSE. Hoping to wire to Lynn and heartened by some politicians and civil servants, NSE took soundings. The council saw the value of slashing 124-minute Lynn–London journeys to 100 minutes and feared the negativity of shuttles. Backed by socio-economic analysis, consultations and lobbying, an intense campaign followed. MPs, MEPs, user group and media were on board. On 6 April 1988 the council offered an electrification revenue guarantee of £650,000 over six years. Other Cambridgeshire and Norfolk councils plus local industry pledged further support. A high-powered delegation presented an evidence-based case to the minister on 11 May 1988.

A 'supplementary' appraisal of 15 November 1988 made a financial case for *hourly* London–Lynn 321s, regardless of whether Peterborough depot was used (best returns) or not. Six options were tested, including a new 'hybrid' – detaching/attaching a DMU to a 321 at Cambridge to keep through trains. Experimental Class 210 DEMUs of 1982 were compatible with some EMUs and perhaps these were envisaged. Runners-up to hourly were 321s to Lynn on existing frequencies, or – if Peterborough depot had already closed – the 'hybrid'.

Peterborough depot was considered 'key' and external funding essential. Existing signalling would be immunised; Ely remodelling/resignalling would become a separate project. The earlier appraisal's assumption of 6 miles of double-track reinstatement (north of Littleport for 1 mile, and between Magdalen Road and Lynn) was deemed unnecessary. Seven new 321/3s were also included (these never turning a wheel on the line).

The Clapham rail disaster (12 December 1988) occurred in the week that authorisation was expected. Understandably, it didn't materialise. 'No train set for Christmas' said the Borough Council's chief executive. Anxious weeks followed until approval came on 7 February 1989. That May, the line was branded part of 'Anglia Electrics'. Clapham forced the safety pace – full Ely remodelling/resignalling was authorised on 2 July 1990.

An upbeat meeting on 23 July 1990 saw top NSE management setting out strategy. The target opening date was May 1992, and the headline Lynn–London journey time just ninety-nine minutes. The ultimate aim was a ninety-minute journey to London, signalling controlled from Cambridge, and a 'couple' of extra loops on the single lines.

Another accident (Newton, 31 July 1991) diverted signalling staff and resources from the Ely scheme, causing delays. When at 11.15 on 28 July 1992 HM The Queen Mother inaugurated electrification at Lynn, the EMU she named *King's Lynn Festival* could not have moved far! Hourly electric operations on the 41 miles between Cambridge and Lynn had to wait until late August. Congestion on the Liverpool Street line, exacerbated by Stansted Airport services since 19 March 1991, meant most services took the faster King's Cross route.

In brief: 2,085 pieces of steel uprights, 2,009 foundations, 92 tension lengths and 24 main permanent way stages, work ending with Ely remodelling/resignalling.

From 1 April 1994 the service was rebranded West Anglia Great Northern (WAGN). On 29 May nonstop Cambridge–Kings Cross runs, marketed as 'Cambridge Cruiser' (later 'Cambridge Express'), were launched, and over half continued to/from Lynn. WAGN was privatised on 5 January 1997.

First Capital Connect (FCC) took over on 1 April 2006. By then peak services were overcrowded. Upgrade plans were developed in 2011 by Network Rail (NR). The line's then six stations north of Cambridge topped four million users in 2014. Govia Thameslink Railway (GTR, operating as Great Northern, GN) started on 14 September that year. Its franchise stipulated half-hourly Lynn–Kings Cross trains from May 2017. That month Cambridge North opened, and it and Ely gained half-hourly trains.

Power upgrading in 2018 preceded longer platforms at Littleport and Waterbeach, and a new stabling siding at Lynn. Regular GN eight-car operation started on 13 December 2020, Waterbeach gaining half-hourly services.

Ely is East Anglia's rail crossroads. Congested with no room for growth, far-reaching works are needed before more trains operate. In autumn 2021, NR consultations on the 'Ely Area Capacity Enhancement' (EACE) programme suggested two double junctions, bi-directional running on all tracks, plus road works (bridge or new road). Unblocking Ely has strong support across the political spectrum. Consultations continue, no half-hourly to Lynn yet!

Approvals for new stations at Cambridge South and Waterbeach (relocation) have been granted.

As well as GN, Greater Anglia (GA) runs on the line with Liverpool Street–Cambridge North services. A few extend to Ely, one peak extra runs to Lynn. CrossCountry (XC) and GA run other services over the line too; East Midlands Railway dips in and out of Ely. Freight operators and Ely steam specials provide more variety.

Cambridge–Lynn was included in both Thameslink 2000 and Intercity Express Programme proposals. Neither came to fruition as envisaged, but associated 700s and 800s sometimes run over all or part of the line. 'ECML Outer-suburban' or 'Intercity'? The Government has previously floated transferring the King's Cross–Lynn service to LNER. GTR currently has a National Rail contract until 1 April 2025.

The September 1999 timetable had the best off-peak London–Lynn time - ninety-three minutes. This had increased to ninety-seven minutes (including Cambridge North) when the May 2018 'Transforming Rail' timetable, linking GN with Thameslink, restructured things drastically. Overnight, journeys increased by twelve minutes, to 109 minutes! Fluctuating needs for twelve cars south of Cambridge mean up to eight minutes can be scheduled for attaching/detaching there. The ECML timetable recast (intended for May 2022, not yet implemented) would cut timetabled northbound waits of up to seven minutes at Littleport, with off-peak London–Lynn journeys of 101 minutes.

King's Lynn or Kings Lynn? Before 1911 the station was Lynn Town, sometimes simply Lynn. In this book it's mostly Lynn. Bishop's Stortford, Downham Market, Great Ouse, Queen Adelaide and Stow Bardolph (Stow Bridge) are similarly shortened. Incidentally, London services mean that Kings Cross and Liverpool Street feature occasionally.

These photographs are chronological, showing construction scenes as well as everyday operations over much of the thirty-year period and the years before it. Professional, later voluntary interests often gave me privileged vantage points for photography. Not all pictures are in perfect sunlit conditions (some far from those) but I hope our journey in all weathers and conditions will be enjoyable. Finally, the Potters Bar catastrophe, 10 May 2002. An unexplained, unforgotten tragedy.

Inevitably, there will have been developments since this book was completed (when the December 2022 timetable was in operation). Most notably, the May 2023 timetable was expected to see the withdrawal of Greater Anglia operations between Ely and Lynn and an extended Great Northern half-hourly Lynn–London peak pattern introduced.

Many have helped with this book, in different ways, often unknowingly. Thank you. Errors are mine. I'm particularly grateful for the outstanding support and encouragement of my family, Mark Collins, Steve Smithson, and Mark Steele through more than three decades of photography.

Recommended organisations:
The line users group – flua.org.uk
Branch Line Society – branchline.uk
Network SouthEast Railway Society – nsers.org

Regardless of recently singled sections north of Ely, this 1986 Cambridge view of a blue '47 with nine on' about to cross over into Platform No. 1 suggests business as usual. NSE was established on 10 June, yet BR's InterCity map still includes Lynn. Wires were coming from the south; 08529 trundles past an electrification train.

Liverpool Street–Stortford electrics had run since 1960. On 16 March 1987 a DMU waits at Stortford Platform No. 3 to form the 15.15 all stations to Cambridge connection. EMU 305507, right, had departed Liverpool Street at 14.08 on a slow. The DMU also connected here with the 14.35 Liverpool Street–Lynn express.

A few electrics ran to Cambridge from 19 January 1987. During late March/early April 305504 had arrived in Platform No. 2 with a Liverpool Street stopper. Full Liverpool Street electrics would commence in May. The DMU shuttle in Platform No. 3 is for Royston (electrics from Royston to Kings Cross since 1978).

From 11 May 1987, locos, not passengers, changed at Cambridge. The 81 has brought the very first electric 'The Fenman' (16.35 from Liverpool Street) and uncoupled. Diesel 47583 *County of Hertfordshire*, distantly seen near Mill Road bridge, will back onto the Lynn-bound train standing in Platform No. 4. That day, Norwich and Peterborough went electric too.

NSE made its mark with at least one re-liveried carriage on each route from the start. By 26 May 1987 its brightness was spreading. The DMU shuttle from Cambridge meets 317371 at Royston. On the route of the former 'Cambridge Buffet Expresses', passengers change for Kings Cross.

It was time for me to go over to colour, for in May 1987 much of the old remained to be photographed at Lynn. The hired-in Provincial DMU arriving from Ely is in blue/grey, the March-allocated 08 and the 47 are in blue. Lynn is 99 miles from Kings Cross, 97 from Liverpool Street.

Except on Sundays, InterCity hired NSE its 'East Anglian' set for a return to Lynn and back between Norwich–London peak duties. On 11 July 1987 the 13.00 from Lynn (buffet only on Saturdays, full restaurant Mondays to Fridays) waits to depart Downham.

About twenty-five minutes later, 31466 brings 1920 GER balcony saloon No. 1 with Railway Heritage Trust (RHT) and senior railway managers past the 1881 Grade II listed box. Downham's 1846 Grade II listed station buildings restoration and electrification were discussed as the train was propelled Up towards Ely.

A grey summer's day – the 47 will stop just short of the crossover and passengers disembark. It will then draw forward, the ground frame will be employed, the loco will then run round using the run-round road. The stock will be propelled towards the stops, ready for the next departure.

It's 24 September 1987 at Cambridge and I have attached the Borough Council's 'The Fenman' headboard on the front of 86246 *Royal Anglian Regiment* with a putty-like adhesive for a publicity shot. Genuine loco, fake working – minus board, it departed Platform No. 1 with the 11.05 Liverpool Street.

The Gala Day bunting was out at Royston on bank holiday Monday 2 May 1988 to celebrate 'Cambridge–Kings Cross goes electric'. One of the celebratory free Cambridge–Royston shuttles arrives at Royston with 317372. Normal Kings Cross–Cambridge electric services started on 16 May.

The bracketed semaphore at Ely symbolises simplification – it once served the lifted Down Main. Provincial-liveried 'Sprinter' 150123 on the Down Platform Road calls on its way to Birmingham New Street on 7 May 1988. The 1880 Ely North box controlled the level crossing gates.

Over at Back Platform No. 3 that same 1988 day, 'Sprinter' 156411 in revised Provincial livery waits to depart for Peterborough. The Norwich-bound DMU typifies the old. The 'Sprinter revolution' saw many more services reversing here, each one taking two paths through Ely North Junction.

Electrification was approved on 7 February 1989. Come 2 May, 31240 and 31247, both in Railfreight grey/yellow, were powering a heavy Up train with silica sand from Middleton Towers towards the bowstring Ouse Bridge, located on the single-line section between Downham and Littleport.

Entering Littleport, the 13.00 Lynn–Cambridge that day is formed of two 101 DMUs. The platform shelter (here flanked by NSE red lamp posts and later destroyed by fire on 3 April 2005) is all that remained of the Cambridgeshire station's buildings. Double-track all the way south from here, though the 1992 Ely North Junction remodelling would change that.

The 37s had once been regulars on Liverpool Street expresses. Later on 2 May 1989, Railfreight 37378 hurries the Lynn–March 'Speedlink' through Stow, the mid-point of the Watlington–Downham double-track section. This 'dynamic loop' gives timetabling flexibility as trains can pass at speed.

Red stripe-liveried 20108 and 20215 work the Barrington (Foxton) to Lynn coal empties past the same spot, later still. The hoppers would be tripped by 08s to Lynn docks for loading; the 20s returned light that day.

Magdalen Road box is ex-Great Central, relocated in 1927 by the LNER. Watlington's 1846 station became Magdalen Road in 1875 and closed on 9 September 1968. A vigorous campaign saw reopening on 5 May 1975. On 2 May 1989, 101s work the 17.35 Lynn–Cambridge.

Extons Road sidings at Lynn lie derelict, a signal post in a former road bed. An InterCity-liveried named 47 takes the curve in May 1989. From 15 May, Class 47s ran directly to Liverpool Street with no loco changing at Cambridge.

Electrification work began on 14 August 1989. A public demonstration of intent occurred on 30 August. The crane, match wagon, departmental brake van, bogie flat and standard brake van had spent the night in Lynn yard and now the time had come to plant mast C/156/06.

Following that 'first mast' ceremony, 47581 *Great Eastern* in revised NSE livery hauled a private inauguration special to Cambridge. Time to capture the moment from Downham signal box steps before a Down working clears the single line from Littleport.

On 3 September, a Cambridge-bound 101 arrives at Magdalen Road (ceremoniously renamed Watlington on 30 September). The DMU had travelled over the single line from Lynn. The NSE signal box nameboard and Magdalen Road sign on the original Up Platform contrast with the Down Side GER wooden platform shelter (demolished 1999).

Part of the West Anglia Gala Day on 30 September 1989 brought the first EMU to Lynn. Hauled by 56062, EMU 310057 worked the 'West Anglian Enterprise'. A blue/grey DMU is in Platform No. 2; the other 101 operates the Middleton Towers gala shuttle.

South of the site of the long-gone overbridge carrying the former M&GN main line and of Lynn's former Harbour Junction box (closed 1984), the crane lifts yet another steel frame foundation reinforcement on 2 February 1990. The location is very close to Hatson crossing.

The train that day was in the control of red stripe 31272. Since 14 August the previous year, Lynn–Ely buses had been substituting for off-peak trains between 09.00 and 16.00. Tickets to Kings Cross were also passed on Provincial's Hunstanton–Lynn–Peterborough coach link.

By 23 March, the excavator was working so close behind the main train that from this angle it appears to be part of it. A mile-and-a-half south of the Norfolk/Cambridgeshire boundary (located at Black Horse Drove), 31422 waits, crawls, and waits.

Loco-hauled London peak trains still ran. Regular loco 47581 *Great Eastern* gazes at Liverpool Street rebuilding on 11 April 1990. With the Great Eastern Hotel in the background, the scene breathes GER. However, the GNR Kings Cross route is the fastest!

Lynn–Cambridge workings were being operated frequently with blue/grey 101s such as this arriving at Downham later in April. Platform No. 1 had been lengthened previously – the train is reaching where new and old join. The NSE clock had yet to be commissioned.

Some days later, 47579 *James Nightall GC* (a hero of the 2 June 1944 Soham rail disaster, born in Littleport) waits to depart Lynn. Once used by the South Lynn shuttle, connecting with the M&GN main line, the Down Side bay trackbed is now the overspill car park approach.

During the December 1989–May 1990 timetable, on Sundays buses replaced trains before the first Lynn departure at 13.23. On 6 May 1990 L224 passes new uprights and an operational semaphore at Stow with the 14.15 from Cambridge, the first northbound service.

47581 *Great Eastern* takes the 09.00 on the final loco-hauled train to Liverpool Street. Nearing Extons Road, Lynn, with blue 'Last Official Diesel Kings Lynn Cambridge Liverpool Street 12th May 1990' headboard, it also carries a CURC (Cambridge University Railway Club) device.

Nearest the stops, L221 is in original NSE light blue, L224 at the front in the later, darker version. They are about to work the 11.28 Lynn–Cambridge that historic Saturday. The run-round will soon become redundant. 08538 and 08540 have no work that day.

That afternoon, L220 arrived at Downham Market with the 16.09 Lynn–Cambridge, shortly followed by a double set (L224 at rear) on the 15.43 Cambridge–Lynn entering Platform No. 2. Norfolk's nearest station to London was *officially* 'Downham' until 1 June 1981.

The evening wears on and 47581 *Great Eastern* eases the 18.32 Liverpool Street–Lynn 'Network Express' into Downham. The headboard with 30A, SF and Cockney Sparrow motifs reads 'Farewell Stratford Passenger Locos, Last Scheduled Diesel Service from Liverpool Street 12th May 1990'.

13 May 1990 and *Great Eastern* and sister 47576 *King's Lynn* shared the very last loco-hauled passenger workings, these Sunday services running to Cambridge for onwards connections to London. *King's Lynn* accelerates towards Hardwick Road bridge, Lynn.

Then followed the reign of standard-class-only DMU shuttles between Cambridge and Lynn. In early June 1990 DMU L700 and EMU 317330 with a Kings Cross train symbolise the new – both passengers and traction changed here, at Cambridge. From that summer until 18 March 1991, Stansted Express 322s worked Liverpool Street connections.

No. 4 is the northern part of the long platform at Cambridge, No. 1 being the other end. The glazed bright red span is the 1989 Tony Carter cycle bridge. It's still early June and behind the all-over grey 31 on an electrification train there are three 310s.

Departing from Cambridge No. 4 with plumes of exhaust fumes the same day, two-car L221 heads two similar units. The six-car DMU formation has made the Lynn connection off the 317 EMU from Kings Cross, just visible in No. 1.

Probably what was Lynn's first regular passenger service EMU ran on 17 June 1990. No wires, so EMU 310077, substituting for a failed DMU, was hauled by 31428 *North York Moors Railway*. The pair, operating the 17.35 from Cambridge and 19.24 return, found the run-round loop useful.

By summer, works trains were getting quite common. In bay Platform No. 2, 08540 heads an electrification train including a cement mixer and rail-mounted excavator. The tail lamp marker stands by DMU L831.

The wiring train had been stabled overnight in Downham Back Road (closed 20 July 1992) and on 27 September 1990 31402 arrived to collect it. The loco propels the train southwards, 'wrong road'. The barrow crossing was still operational (closed 9 May 2011), the bracketed signal post not.

A little later, 31402 was still pushing the train, now in fits and starts. It's stationary at Hilgay Fen on the Downham–Littleport single line as workers assemble overhead wires. Daylight working saved costs; replacement Lynn–Ely buses were running.

The wiring train variously moved in both directions as work unfolded on 27 September 1990. Having emptied the sole cable drum, 31402 is seen at the Cut-off Channel bridge, returning temporarily to Downham. The former Down Main road bed can be seen.

Back from Downham, the wiring train moved Up and Down relevant sections, seen here crawling northwards across the Ouse bridge. Converted ex-LMS coach LDM395691, built in Derby in 1925, makes sure we know it's on electrification business!

Day's work finished, another empty cable drum; 31402 pulls the wiring train northwards past the white sails of distant Denver mill. Line possession will be handed back on arrival at Downham and the 'Speedlink' trip working to March waiting there can depart.

There were fine displays of locos and stock at both Cambridge and Lynn on 29 September 1990 when the second West Anglia Gala Day was held. The rain came as activities were finishing at Lynn. Displays included 45133 and 'Dutch'-liveried 31541.

Lynn Platform No. 2 road has been realigned and the Down Side bay track already removed. The date fixed for Tennyson Avenue footbridge's demolition was 13 January 1991. Shortly before it came down, L225 leaves Lynn for Cambridge.

In February or March, L831 arrives at Lynn as 47346 sits in the realigned Platform No. 2 Road with a communications cable train. Platform No. 2 itself is still in its unextended state, curving away sharply at its eastern end, and reflects the old arrangements.

The south end of Ely on 26 April 1991. Ely South box had long gone (closed 29 June 1985). The former turnout for the Down Platform Road was replaced by a plain reverse curve when the Down Main was removed; the semaphores echo the old arrangements. L221 waits to shuttle back to Lynn.

On 9 May 1991 semaphores rule at Lynn too. Framed between the starters, L700 approaches the station under the wires. The discarded footbridge span lurks to the left. The loco fuelling point, demolished in May 1994, remains to service two Cambridge-allocated 08 shunters.

The road serving the freight dock at Lynn, seen here on 9 May with 31402 resting between duties, was also wired, though this work had yet to be completed. There is copper on one of the cable drums. At the line's southern end, Cambridge (including Platforms Nos 5/6) to Waterbeach North was energised from 08.30 on 30 June.

Following attendance at the gala day on 14 September, RHDR No. 1 *Green Goddess* of 1924 was soon back at Lynn for the 'Fen Line Steam Weekend'. Big cousin 4472 *Flying Scotsman* visited too. The RHDR was setting up for the weekend as coal hoppers are shunted by 08713 past the new EMU Wash on Friday 18 October 1991.

Next day, another distinguished guest, 'West Country' 4-6-2 34027 *Taw Valley*, carrying both 'Golden Arrow' and 'The Fenman' headboards, brings one of the weekend's specials past the 1882 Kings Lynn Junction signal box.

Attached to the rear of *Taw Valley*'s train was DMU L220 on a Cambridge–Lynn service, the only way to path both over the single lines. Regular passengers couldn't alight as the combined train was too long, so waiting 08495 collected the DMU and shunted it to Platform No. 2.

Sunday 20 October 1991 saw more 08 work with the 'Queen of Scots' stock, normally stabled in Lynn for use on Duke's Head Hotel dining specials. Fourth Steam Weekend star 70000 *Britannia*, which took King George VI's funeral train from Lynn to Kings Cross on 11 February 1952, waits with support coach.

The last time the late Queen Elizabeth II used the Royal Train at Lynn was on 1 July 2022. On 17 January 1992, 47835 *Windsor Castle* in INTERCITY 'Swallow' livery prepares to take the Princess Royal to Newcastle. Disturbing the peace, a gang excavates trenches for the platform extension.

The first timetable draft showed no promised Lynn–Kings Cross 100-minute services. Meanwhile on 15 February there were hourly Lynn–Downham and Littleport–Cambridge shuttles. L220 stands at Littleport waiting for rail replacement buses. The new starter is not yet commissioned.

Later that day, the dolly permits L831 to depart 'wrong direction' from Downham's Up Platform No. 1 and return to Lynn. Downham to Littleport was closed for piling at the River 'Wissey viaduct', quarter of a mile north of Ouse Bridge, eventually lifting its speed capability from 40 mph to 100 mph.

On 15 February 1992, L831 (again) pauses at Watlington Down Platform No. 2, which was being extended. Sister L830, showing 'Special', works to Downham, both on Wissey viaduct shuttles. Up Platform No. 1 is to be relocated northwards, opening on 20 July.

A Cambridge-bound blue/grey 101 passes signs of the end for the Ely North semaphores. It's 28 February 1992 – new track has been placed on the alignment of the former Down Main in anticipation of the future widened Platform No. 1. The box would be demolished by 29 April.

The line has been temporarily shifted to the former Down Main formation to permit work on the seven-span Wissey viaduct, a slue just visible in the run towards the Ouse Bridge. By 22 April, the 'permanent way' is wired, bridge-mounted portal mast C/134/03 being located directly above the river.

NSE's revised service proposition had nineteen Up and eighteen Down London trains, many taking 100 minutes. Between 11 April and 10 May 1992 the Ely area shut for remodelling. On 25 April, the 1928 Ely Dock Junction box was disappearing.

Ely North Junction box of 1926 still stood on 25 April 1992 as the crane lifts track panels. Two double junctions came out, bi-directional working, and two single leads went in – the Lynn and Norwich roads leaving the double-track Peterborough route as just a single common line before diverging and each becoming double.

Double-headed 31s in engineer's grey/yellow 'Dutch' livery haul spoil at Ely North Junction that day. During the four-week blockade, buses ran between Downham/Littleport to Cambridge (to Ely from 9 May). Regional Railways (Provincial renamed, from 1991) used Shippea Hill and a temporary Chettisham station for train/bus transfers on east–west routes.

Everything nearly in place at Ely on 9 May 1992, when trains to Cambridge restarted (every other extended to Stansted Airport). L221 stands where the relocated Down Main now serves Platform No. 1. The new layout allows for faster transit. Platforms were lengthened to take twelve cars; as at Cambridge and Lynn, splitting/joining would be permitted here.

Watlington's new Platform No. 1, left, seen on 16 August as L830 departs. 25kV had been live between St Germans North and Lynn since 00.01 on 1 July. HM The Queen Mother had named 317361 *King's Lynn Festival* on 28 July at Lynn's refurbished station. Waterbeach North to St Germans North had been energised from 00.01 on 3 August.

Pausing at 13.33 alongside the elegant curved canopy brackets at Downham (part of the RHT renewal) on 18 August 1992, EMU 302998 with the Up proving train waits for the single line to clear. Load bank tests had taken place on the nights of 11 August (three 317s) and 12/13 August (two 90s with overhead line test coach *Mentor*).

L830 waits at Lynn with the 09.43 Lynn–Cambridge on Saturday 22 August. 'West Anglia'-badged eight-car EMUs 317309 and 317312 arrive from Cambridge, showing 'Special'. That day DMUs ran one-way to Cambridge and EMUs took over services from/to Cambridge on existing timings.

The first electrics through to London ran on 24 August, the first three to Liverpool Street. The Borough Mayor flagged off the next, the 07.08 'The Fenman' to Kings Cross. The Cambridge MP flagged the 06.40 from Kings Cross away from Cambridge. This picked up the Mayors of Ely and Downham en route. Lynn on 29 August hosts 317311, 317367 and another 317.

EMUs, such as 317312 and 317311 (front), at rebuilt Liverpool Street on 25 September 1992, carried headboards for some weeks. 'The Fen Line Limited' name didn't last as long as the 'The Fenman', which appeared in timetables. The refreshment trolley is being unloaded.

Rounded front 317353 contrasts with original design 317336 at the rear of the eight-car 10.45 for Lynn on 13 October 1992 in Kings Cross main train shed Platform Nos 7/8. Eight-car services could not stop at short-platformed Waterbeach, Littleport and Watlington.

The eight-car 08.40 Kings Cross–Lynn, near Stow on 28 October, will shortly cross the four-car 10.03 from Lynn. Holding late-running Down trains at Watlington allowed time-sensitive London-bound services priority on the single line from Lynn. Most workings became four-car all-stations services from 1 June 1997.

'Express Sprinter' 158793 arrives at Ely from Peterborough on 19 November 1992. Its Yarmouth destination means it will traverse Ely North Junction twice. It carries a guard – the 317s went Driver Only Operation (DOO) on 30 November. Tamper/Liner DR73801 stands on the then Engineers' Stabling Road.

Lynn's extended platform in the damp on 27 February 1993. 317s occupy both platforms. The stock of INTERCITY's 'The North Norfolkman' rail tour, 09.00 off Kings Cross, sits with 47819 in Carriage Siding No. 1. In the station, slow-speed tram wire (no catenary) is used, supported by headspans.

Demonstrator 'Networker Express' third-rail 465301 (modified unit 465037) was exhibited on 26 July 1993 at Cambridge Platform No. 6, alongside amusingly numbered 317317. The 465 visited Ely, towed by 317367, for gauging trails on 28 November.

In mid-winter 1993/4, 317331 leaves Lynn for Kings Cross as 58047 *Manton Colliery* waits with a sand train. The second train will move when the first reaches the next block, both clearing the single line in time for the scheduled Down working to occupy it.

Liverpool Street is the West Anglia destination; Kings Cross the Great Northern. Routes were combined in the new pre-privatisation unit's WAGN name. On 20 September 1994, Italy wasn't the terminus for the 'Venice Simplon Orient Express' Sandringham tour – here at Lynn with 47770 *Reserved*.

As 317354 waits departure, 365501 is the new arrival on 27 February 1996, the second day of 'Networker' trials. Railtrack was undertaking CCTV monitoring equipment and platform clearance works; WAGN posters promised mid-April completion. Unlike Lynn's usual cascaded stock, 365s were brand new.

All three platform roads at Ely are bi-directional. Bound for Lynn on a murky 23 March, 317369 approaches the island platform. The 'Welcome to Ely' sign advertises BR-owned WAGN. Come July, Cambridge–Lynn would be included in the Trans European Network.

Another overcast day, 9 August. NSE colours are dominating at Cambridge where 317355 arrives in Platform No. 4. The scissors crossover provides operational flexibility for combined Platform Nos 1/4. In the sidings, 317350 bears the blue, gold and white WAGN motif, the triangles representing Peterborough, Lynn and London.

The fog was no deterrent to photography on 6 December 1996 as 365524 arrives at Downham during the second week of Hitchin–Lynn driver training on the new dual-voltage EMUs. WAGN would become privatised shortly, on 5 January 1997.

Warranties precluded 365s being re-liveried. In 1998/9 WAGN refurbished 317s in a yellow-and-blue-banded white livery, seen at Lynn. The 17 October 2000 fatal Hatfield accident slowed ECML services greatly, Kings Cross–Lynn included. This 'Gauge Corner Cracking Crisis' was prolonged. As a consequence, Railtrack was superseded by NR.

From 2001, WAGN (sold by Prism Rail to National Express in July 2000) adopted a purple livery. Thus coloured, a 317 watches 365514 arrive at Cambridge. The service's worst nightmare happened on 10 May 2002, when 365526, approaching Potters Bar with the 12.45 Kings Cross–Lynn, derailed at about 100 mph with seven fatalities.

Some regular Norwich–London services ran via Ely in the 1950s and the 1980s. During the eight-week summer 2004 Ipswich tunnel blockade, a peak working came that way again. Cotswold Rail 47818 in 'One' livery passes Ely West River (Little Thetford) with a push-pull set in Anglia colours on the 06.30 Norwich–Liverpool Street. (Steve Smithson)

One was an amalgamation of Anglia, First Great Eastern and WAGN's West Anglia services from 1 April 2004. In its coat of many colours, 317670 contrasts with newcomer FCC's 365513 at Lynn on 16 September 2007. The fitting of cab air-conditioning resulted in revised 365 front ends, complete with 'smile'. (Brian Beckett)

Central Trains ran until 12 November 2007. Central's 170519 on an afternoon Stansted–Birmingham New Street service crosses into Cambridge Platform No. 4 on 19 September that year. Ely and Cambridge stations were operated by One at that time, as was 317662 (right). (Brian Beckett)

On 5 March 2009, 365502 arrives at Waterbeach. The 1985 Automatic Half Barrier (AHB) does not protect the pedestrian route to Up Platform No. 1, hidden behind the EMU. On 12 September 2013 a cyclist narrowly avoided disaster here. Approval for full barriers was sought on 5 August 2022 as part of the 'Cambridge Resignalling, Relock & Recontrol' (C3R) project.

National Express rebranded One as National Express East Anglia in February the year before. On 2 August 2009, 317671, stabled at Lynn, demonstrates how this 'NXEA' livery required removal of One's many colours plus a plain white stripe along the side.

Heading northwards on 18 December 2009, 365534 throws up snow. There are two long sections of portals between Adelaide and Littleport. FCC inherited a merged WAGN/Thameslink operation: the Thameslink 2000 scheme was intended to include Cambridge to King's Lynn. (Steve Smithson)

In its blue FCC 'Urban Lights' livery, 365539 passes spoil heaps as island platform work at Cambridge progresses on 23 August 2011. This would be the third island platform; the other two came and went in Victorian days! The Lynn–Kings Cross train will use the scissors crossover to reach Platform No. 1 from the Through Line. The XC 'Turbostar' 170 in Platform No. 4 is for Birmingham New Street.

First-of-class 365501 at Lynn on 29 September. Like the 317s before them, the 365s' 100 mph capability was useful on the 32-mile ECML dash from Cambridge Junction, Hitchin, to Kings Cross, with trains normally using the Fast Lines.

A few days later, on 5 October 2011, 365529 leaves Cambridge Platform No. 1 with the 13.56 Lynn–Kings Cross. NXEA 317663 and FCC 321420 wait in the southern bay platforms. Those seven new 321/3s approved in 1989 went to the West Coast Main Line; those used between Cambridge and Kings Cross were built earlier.

The new Cambridge footbridge connects to future Platform Nos 7/8 (opened 12 December 2011), where steelwork for the new canopy is already in place that day. Recently arrived 170639 on a Birmingham New Street service, next stop Ely, attracts a crowd. In late December 2022, a safety barrier was erected along the platform edge to prevent people falling onto the track at the often heavily congested spot where Platform Nos 1 and 4 meet.

On 25 September 1T60 10.10 Lynn–Ely had struck a tractor at 70 mph at Hatson Crossing, 2 miles south of Lynn. There had been a communications misunderstanding. Damaged 365532 was taken to the refuge siding at Downham, seen there on 5 October 2011. Passing on service are 365514, centre, and 365538, right.

Ticket gates were installed at Lynn over ten weeks from 13 February 2012 – about the time when a fake ticket collector was roaming! On 10 March, 365531 promotes 'Norfolk – Nelson's County'. The unit had been launched by WAGN at Lynn on 29 September 2005. Standing in Platform No. 2 is 365513 *Hornsey Depot* (principal maintenance depot for the line).

Kings Cross on 18 July 2012 – 365505, the 11.45 Lynn express, and 365520, the 11.53 Cambridge semi-fast. The eight-car 365, far right, was the early 09.59 from Lynn (front unit attaching at Cambridge). Since the 2021 'Kings Cross Uncrossed' remodelling, the centre track is disused. These 'suburban' platforms lead onto the 2012 semi-circular concourse.

FCC started the heritage-inspired Lynn station refurbishment on 11 April 2013, this opening ceremoniously on 22 July 2014. Posing by a new sign on 2 April 2014, 365517 *Supporting Red Balloon* (a charity) is in new colours itself, ready for the transition to GN from 14 September.

GN 365510 in Cambridge bay Platform No. 6 on 5 October 2016 with the 16.19 Cambridge–Downham 'schools train'. No time for a Littleport call – it had to be at Downham punctually to cross the 16.36 Lynn–Kings Cross (departure due at 16.51). Then it was due to shunt, wait for the 15.44 from Kings Cross (due 17.10) and be away sharpish as the 17.10 Downham–Kings Cross.

Later on, the four-car 365 operating the 16.36 Lynn–Kings Cross runs in under the Tony Carter bridge, before crossing over to reach Platform No. 1. Confusion over the two Kings, Cross and Lynn, reigns at Cambridge; attaching/detaching units required 'when the train divides at Platform No. 4, the carriages beyond this point are for Kings Lynn boards.'

Not permitted north of Milton neutral section are twelve-car EMUs and electric locos 'with pantograph raised'. Only five four-car units in total were allowed until upgrading. A Down working with 365530 in charge slows as it approaches Waterbeach, some 3 miles north of Milton, on a damp 10 December 2016. (Jill Beckett)

On 14 February 2017 the shunter on Cambridge Platform No. 1 uses his radio to advise the driver of 365505, right, to set back and couple to 365501, left, which has arrived from Lynn. The combined train will go forward to Kings Cross as an eight-car set.

The Royal Papworth Hospital (blue building, seen under construction) joins Addenbrooke's Hospital at the Cambridge Biomedical Campus. The Medical Research Council block is just north of Addenbrooke's Bridge, under which 365538, heading a Kings Cross train, has just passed later that day.

The key to working Cambridge is the scissors crossover. Dutch-style, this permits very flexible working of combined Platform Nos 1/4. On 24 April 2017, 365523 in No. 4, left, waits to form the 15.24 Cambridge–Ely while 365539, right, sits with the 15.15 Cambridge–Kings Cross at No. 1. GA 100 mph 'Electrostar' 379030 approaches No. 7.

The next day saw plenty of April showers! Ely Platform No. 1 canopy covers just the original structure and not that part situated over the former Down Platform Road. Passengers alight as others join XC 170105 off to Birmingham New Street.

Three generations of EMU at Lynn on 21 May. Enjoying the sun are 387106, in front of 387108, left; GA red-doored 317505, centre; and 365523 in Platform No. 1, right. 'Electrostar' 110 mph 387s were first tested at Lynn on 14 January 2017 (at night) and 7 April 2017 (daytime).

On 21 May 2017 Cambridge North's first trains included 379008 on the 16.44 Liverpool Street in the vastness of the former Chesterton Junction yard. Half-hourly Lynn services should have started that day, only 'Ely terminators' did. Cambridge 'Parkway' was an EMU destination display, but 'North' was the name chosen. It opened ceremonially on 7 August.

It's 1 June and 387021 moves southwards away from the approved site for the relocated Waterbeach station. Due to open in 2025, there will be two eight-car platforms (protected extension for twelve cars) and two covered footbridges. Waterbeach's population is likely to expand six-fold.

GA 170273 wears adapted former Anglia colours on 29 June 2017. May should have seen hourly Ipswich–Peterborough trains too. The Ely 'bottleneck' – accommodating north–south and east–west flows – is signalled bi-directionally, but still cannot handle more traffic.

People scurry to join 387107 at Lynn on 28 February 2018. Unbranded 317339 with GN light-blue doors had failed earlier and its GA Liverpool Street service was cancelled. It stands in Carriage Siding No. 2.

That snowy day 387109 crosses 387107 at Downham. The May 2018 'Transforming Rail' changes would link Thameslink and GN services. Instead of Downham, Littleport became the new crossing point, slowing northbound journeys. However, overall, the changes were overambitious and caused widespread cancellations and delays.

The first 700 in service to Ely ran on 26 March 2018. 'Desiro City' 700056 stands on layover on 6 April before working the 10.58 Ely–Kings Cross. Colas Rail's Plasser & Theurer 08-16/4X4C-RT tamper DR73912 *Lynx* hides in the Engineers' Siding, left.

The cathedral overshadows 387107 at the rear of a static 'Ely terminator' on 26 June. All Ely's platforms take twelve cars; the eight-car is positioned to allow a reversing train on the Norwich–Liverpool Lime Street route to occupy Platform No. 3's northern end.

Four days later, 66120 heads south through Watlington with a loaded sand train. Watlington's staggered platforms, designed to avoid stationary trains fouling the level crossing, provide context for the closure of the former Up Platform, now privately owned.

Ely station bridge was infamous for lorry strikes; the A142 bypass has rerouted traffic. The level crossing was closed on 1 November. Works on the underpass (opened 28 February the following year) were proceeding on 18 December 2018 as 387106 leaves for Lynn.

Construction of Cambridge Carriage Sidings Nos 3–7 was necessitated by fixed-formation Thameslink 700s working Kings Cross semi-fasts and slows as well as cross-London runs to Brighton. A long-reach cement pour is in operation on 10 May 2019. The East–West Rail scheme could see a new platform built this side of the station.

Opened 16/17 October 1982, pitched-roof Cambridge Power Signal Box (PSB) was intended to control Ely–Lynn. GA 379s, like Stansted Express 379028 seen on 10 May 2019, worked Liverpool Street services, including peak Lynn trains. The 379s are now stored. Cambridge's 1845 Grade II listed station was extensively refurbished in 2016/7.

The internationally important freight route from the Midlands and North to Felixstowe includes the 2-mile 'bottleneck' between Ely North Junction and Ely Dock Junction. GB Railfreight 66707 *Sir Sam Fay/Great Central Railway* powers a container train over the speed-restricted Cutter Bridge and through Ely station on 18 May.

Standing at Kings Cross on 15 June is 387114 with the 13.42 Lynn. Only 387114 will go forward at Cambridge, the rear unit detaching there. Revived LNER's new bi-mode 'Azuma' stock is represented by 800111. Stranger 43020 *MTU Power Passion Partnership* is on hire to LNER from First Great Western.

A Kings Cross–Ely service with 387123 passes GBRf 66745 *Modern Railways – The First 50 Years* with a heavy freight in the Through Siding on 1 August 2019. The A142 bypass Bridge BGK1563 opened on 31 October 2018; its approach ramp is in the background. BGK is the Engineers' Line Reference (ELR) for the Bethnal Green–King's Lynn WAML.

The 'Cambridge Railway Sidings Capacity' project required the opening of a new arch under Mill Road bridge, which closed to vehicles between 1 July and 25 August 2019. On 13 August the 14.12 Kings Cross–Ely (eight cars, no Waterbeach call!) is powered by 387115 and 387114.

Accelerating the 13.44 Lynn–Kings Cross southwards on 10 October, 387125 passes the 1882 Littleport signal box, which fringes with Cambridge PSB. Shoring highlights poor ground conditions! The 'King's Lynn Service Enhancement' eight-car upgrade had started five days earlier.

Lynn on Saturday 12 October 2019 and 387119 arrives on a shuttle from Downham. Shuttles ran that weekend with buses onwards to Cambridge North, a better transfer point than congested Cambridge. On the right is 387107 in front of GA 317885.

The same day, Waterbeach-Dosen Ultra Heavy Lift 99709 910104-7 (on the Down Main, left) Manitou Mobile Elevating Working Platform (MEWP) 99709 912135-9 (Up Main, centre) and MEWP 99709 912077-3 (Down Main, right) install new portals. The white covered piles (foreground) will support the Down Platform No. 2 extension.

Looking south from Burgess Drove User Worked Crossing towards Waterbeach station (Platform No. 2 just visible, centre). The Dosen and the MEWP on the Up Main co-operate to lift one of the new uprights into place. Both these types of plant are Road Rail Vehicles (RRVs).

Still 12 October 2019, now Littleport. Volker Rail's Colmar T10000FS RRV Excavator Crane 99709 940786-5 stands on the Up Road, flat wagon 99709 020077-2 on the Down Road. Behind the crossing gates, a road crane manoeuvres sheet piling, preparing for a new Up Platform passenger access ramp.

At Littleport station RRV excavator cranes, 99709 940786-4 (left) and 99709 940786-5 (right) are placing new portal uprights on piles previously sunk into the poor ground. Down Platform No. 2 could not be extended until the work that side was complete.

Lynn, 2 November 2019. Two Colmar T10000FS RRV excavator cranes (the nearer obscuring the other) are on the Middleton 'sand' line (its ELR is MIT). The eight-car Stabling Siding will run parallel to this; the turnout from the Up & Down Road will be installed close to the 30 mph sign.

Weekend bus substitution was now regular. Parked EMUs 387104 and 387129 are seen at Lynn the following day. Prior to universal eight-car platforms, an anti-crowding measure was to run two portions, combining at Cambridge – for example, the 07.05 four-car all-stations and the 07.16 eight-car semi-fast (both from Lynn) combined at Cambridge and ran as twelve cars to Kings Cross.

Kings Lynn Junction box oversees the Manual Controlled Barriers (MCB) at Tennyson Avenue. On 5 November, the rear of 387123 passes the old footbridge site, having already passed the crossover connecting the Up & Down and the 3-mile-long 'sand' lines. DB 66174 is in the yard.

The train standing at Waterbeach Down Platform No. 2 is not going very far! Balfour Beatty's Matisa B41UE tamper DR75408, built 2010, is attending to the remodelled tracks on 9 November 2019. Both old and replacement portal structures are in place.

Cambridge North's cladding has patterns drawn from the Cambridge-invented 'Game of Life' cellular automaton. The new hotel (opened 2021) overshadows the distant footbridge on 28 November. Partnering unseen 317654 *Richard Wells*, 317671 waits with the 11.14 Liverpool Street (now a 720 duty) in No. 3.

Global company Sibelco uses several different hauliers for Middleton sand traffic. DB 66070 is handling matters on drizzly 17 December 2019. There are two run-round loops in Lynn yard, plus a cripple siding. The ELR for this part of the former docks branch is, well... DOC.

Passengers wait to join Stagecoach East Midlands Trains 158846 at Ely Platform No. 3 on 11 January 2020. The 1845 station was upgraded (with RHT involvement) and gated in 2021, completion being on 5 September. It sits on an embankment, above the floodplain.

Bi-mode 755421 on 1K66 09.48 Stansted Airport–Norwich hurries past a dismantled emergency crossover at Waterbeach on 18 January, pan up. Initially GA's 755s had to use diesel mode on the line, faintly echoing the earlier 'hybrid' appraisal option.

Echoes too of past ECML diversions (Deltics, HSTs, etc). Shortly afterwards a LNER bi-mode 800/1 takes 1E02 05.48 Edinburgh–Kings Cross round the curve (greatly exaggerated) towards Waterbeach Down Platform No. 2's extension. The 'Intercity Express Programme ECML Phase 2' had envisaged five-car 801s to Lynn.

GBRf 66776 *Joanne* passes the unfinished Littleport Down Platform extension, 2 minutes late on 29 January 2020, hauling sand empties from Doncaster Roberts Road. The old and replacement portals can be seen, as can the extant barrow crossing.

Next day, 387117 calls at Downham with the 14.44 Lynn–Kings Cross. Passengers now cross via the 1975 MCB. On 21 April 2010 a footbridge was refused planning permission on heritage and inclusivity grounds. Part of another RHT upgrade, new NSE-style station signage was launched on 28 April 2017.

Not only a weekend of shuttle buses (via town) for barricaded Tennyson Avenue MCB but no Up & Down Road! Present on 1 February but unseen here, GBRf's 66747 *Made in Sheffield*, 66752 *The Hoosier State*, 66766, 66777 *Annette*, and Colas' tamper DR73912 *Lynx* were busy. So was the RRV crawler multi-purpose excavator with possession of the road bed.

Kings Lynn Junction again, this time on 22 February 2020 – crossing closed, more minibuses. Remote-controlled Geismar PEM/LEM motorised trolleys operate in multiple to lift a track panel; others are being employed to install the new turnout. That weekend the Stabling Siding was connected to the Up & Down Road.

The first day of Littleport's new ramp and underpass was 24 February. There were free refreshments under the subway bridge to celebrate! That day, 387108 decelerates 1T19 09.10 Lynn–Kings Cross towards Platform No. 1. The barrow crossing has gone, as have the old portal structures.

As soon as 1T19 had cleared the single line, GBRf 66782 left Downham with 6E85 08.20 Middleton–Barnby Dun. Littleport's Down Platform gap could not be filled while the barrow crossing was needed, but with the subway operational this work could now be done.

There was major ECML engineering work on 1 March 2020, so 387112 was going only as far as Letchworth Garden City with the 14.26 from Lynn. Both Watlington platform shelters are 1999 structures, the wooden GER shelter on Platform No. 2 being no more.

A safe, well-lit drivers walkway from Lynn station to the new Stabling Siding was required, necessitating revised cable runs. This work is ongoing as 387109 arrives with the late running 13.42 from Kings Cross on 10 March.

Friday 27 March, the second day of 720 testing to Lynn. GA 720509 on 5Q10 09.40 Liverpool Street–Lynn approaches the Great Catchwater Drain, between Adelaide and Littleport. The 'Aventra' is a five-car unit, roughly as long as six 387 cars. It is standard-class only, with 3+2 seating. (Steve Smithson)

Heading southwards over the Great Catchwater Drain on 17 April 2020 is four-car 387118. Lynn–Ely buses had been needed while the six-span viaduct was strengthened and repainted between 12 and 16 February 2018. (Steve Smithson)

COVID-19 lockdowns (services reduced from 23 March) meant only essential workers were travelling on 12 May 2020. Deserted Cambridge sees a 170, twelve-car 700143 (13.28 Cambridge–Gatwick Airport), and 317340. The 12.11 from Kings Cross, departing Cambridge at 13.04, saw just one passenger off at Waterbeach, one at Ely, and seven at Lynn. (Claire Beckett)

DRS 57312 hauling 317659 (plus 317671) on 5E46 11.14 Ilford–Ely Papworth Sidings (Potter's Yard) for storage on 31 July. East Midlands Regional 158856 heads southwards. Long freights need careful regulation through the Ely bottleneck – stopping would foul nearby Kiln Lane AHB. (Steve Smithson)

The first 700/0 test to/from Lynn ran on 4 November 2020. 700034 on 5T95 13.53 to Cambridge Carriage Servicing Depot spent 10 minutes at Littleport (seen by the replacement platform shelter, opened on 11 July 2007). A 'preview' 387 eight-car run on 11 December was followed two days later by regular eight-car 387 workings. (Steve Smithson)

Major works at Kings Cross meant only five platforms in use there for weeks on end. Temporary inter-workings brought 700/0s to Lynn from 26 February 2021. On 19 March, 700055 works the 17.16 Lynn–Cambridge. The late 15.42 Kings Cross–Lynn (387116 at the rear) was turned short as the 17.40 Downham Market–Hornsey empties. (Mark Collins)

Passing Ely Cathedral, 37800 *Cassiopeia* hauls off-lease 365538 as the 11.34 Hornsey–Ely Papworth Sidings through the bottleneck on 14 April 2021. The 365s' 'Anti DOO-monitor glare' purple fronts were fitted after they had left the line. Two of the problems hereabouts are junction layouts, which impede parallel movements, and speed-restricted bridges. (Steve Smithson)

Cambridge Platform No. 4 was extended from 22 November 2021 to accommodate Liverpool Street–Cambridge North 720s double units. Here at Lynn it's 8 February 2022, the second day of 720s in service further northwards. Having arrived as 5H32 05.20 Cambridge–Lynn empties, 720542 takes out 1H87 06.18 Lynn–Liverpool Street. Carriage Siding No. 1 hosts 387206.

On 15 May 2022 stock in the Lynn eight-car stabling siding (energised from 01.30 on 1 September 2020) consists of 387125 and a red 387/2. They will form 5T53, the 17.44 to Lynn station, then operate 1T53 17.54 to Kings Cross. Some 387/2s were loaned from Gatwick Express from May 2021. Semaphore signal KL8, just visible, left, serves the 'sand' line.

Littleport on 5 June. 1T36 14.12 Kings Cross–Lynn calls, 387122 (visible) trailing 387102. The platformed train is clear of the wooden level crossing gates over Station Road, the former A10. Many Down trains pause here up to 7 minutes, blocked by London-bound Up services on the single line.

At the rear of eight-car 1T43 15.25 Lynn–Kings Cross, 387107 departs Littleport's short Up Platform on 5 June 2022. Up stoppers do not block the crossing, but any rear unit is off the platform. The units are through-gangwayed.

DB 60019 *Port of Grimsby & Immingham* hauls 6Z16 09.10 Chaddesden Sidings–Lynn alongside the Ouse, south of Littleport, on 10 June. These empties will continue the next day as 6Z17 04.50 to Middleton Towers. Booster transformers (white cylinder on portal) militate against voltage drops.

Later, 1T26 11.42 from Kings Cross (with 387115, rear, and 387207 in barely noticeable red leading) enters the Up & Down single line, approaching Littleport neutral section. This is normally the operational division between feeder stations (which transform grid power to 25kV traction current) at Milton and Lynn.

Still 10 June 2022, GBRf 66753 *EMD Roberts Road*, with 6E88 12.26 Middleton Towers–Goole Glassworks, near the Lark/Ouse confluence. On 5 January 2012, the detached pantograph from FCC's 365, working 1T53 06.51 Lynn–Kings Cross, broke a carriage window; this occurred near here. Keeping masts vertical in the peaty soil is an issue.

Ely Dock Junction. 387106 (front) and 387123 (rear) are with 1T34 13.42 Kings Cross–Lynn and 170107 on 1L40 12.22 Birmingham New Street–Stansted Airport pass. DB 66004 'I am a Climate Hero', running on Hydrotreated Vegetable Oil biofuel with the 10.57 East Midlands Gateway–Felixstowe Central containers, and a Down freight are being regulated.

Later on 10 June 2022, XC 170102 operates 1N61 16.00 Cambridge–Birmingham New Street. It's about to enter the 1-mile run of portals, interrupted only by the Ely West River Track Sectioning Location (TSL). The portals start on the approach to West River Bridge, near the Cam/Ouse confluence.

All-red: 387206 (leading) and 387205 crossed A1123 Dimmocks Cote AHB (Stretham) 20 minutes later with 2T92 16.20 Cambridge-Lynn 'schools train'. A drought temporary speed restriction applied here – witness the speed limit 'T' termination board. Approval for full barriers was sought on 5 August 2022, as another element of C3R.

On 16 June 2022, GA five-car 720582 works 1H90 19.07 Liverpool Street–Lynn away from Watlington Road CCTV-monitored crossing (returning as 5H90 21.32 to Cambridge Carriage Sidings South). The second wire on the mast sides along single-line sections transmits current should the contact wire be disrupted and simultaneously a feeder station be 'out'.

The evening wears on and 387126 at the rear of eight-car 1T58 19.39 Kings Cross–Lynn is running 5 minutes down at St Germans. Ahead is the Nar Bridge, from which point masts occupy the former Down Main roadbed as far as Nowhere Crossing, Lynn.

The road sign reads 20 mph. It's 25 mph for trains across Tennyson Avenue MCB. On 3 July 2022 387127 leads 387111 into Lynn with 1T48 17.12 from Kings Cross – 23 minutes late!

A sunny 7 July evening as red 387207 trails a sister 387/2 into Watlington with 1T65 20.44 Lynn–Kings Cross. Right-time presentation onto the four-track ECML at Cambridge Junction, Hitchin, is essential to keep booked paths through the Woolmer Green–Digswell two-track pinch point.

The shadows gather that evening as 387115/387117, headlights ablaze, race towards St Germans. It's 1T58 19.39 Kings Cross–Lynn once again. Northbound trains like this usually exit the ECML at Hitchin by using the 2013 flyover there.

The heatwave had shrunk the peaty soil, causing 'defective track'. On 12 September 2022, 387302 (partnering 387301) heads 1G41 14.44 shuttle to Cambridge; 387106 is in Carriage Siding No. 1. Ely to Kings Cross trains restarted that day, but Lynn to Kings Cross services didn't resume until 5 October.

Colas 37099 *Merl Evans 1947–2016* and 37421 power NR's Plain Line Pattern Recognition Train, 1Q98 14.04 Cambridge Reception Sidings and back (via Norwich, Yarmouth, Lowestoft, and East Suffolk Line) through Milton Fen on 15 September 2022.

Chesterton CCTV-monitored crossing (Fen Road) is just south of Cambridge North. On the same day, 387101 (with 387117 at front) slows for the station call with 1T36 14.12 Kings Cross–Ely. The former St Ives branch (now a Guided Busway) diverged at Chesterton Junction just north of here.

Shortly afterwards, 387122 leads 387121 (rear) on 1T39 14.53 Ely–Kings Cross across the Cam bridge, built in 1931. The parallel Abbey Chesterton cycle bridge, left, dates from November 2020.

Later on 15 September 2022, XC three-car 170103, working 1L42 13.22 Birmingham New Street–Cambridge, passes the former Barnwell Junction. The rail lengths suggest where the former Mildenhall branch, complete with its own station here, later just an oil depot siding, once diverged. 1982 talk of a halt here for football supporters visiting the Abbey Stadium came to nothing.

Still 15 September, at Newmarket Road, Cambridge. Down 1G42 16.35 Cambridge–Lynn (387113 front right) passes the Up 1G45 15.44 Lynn–Cambridge shuttle (387118 trailing 387126, left). An incoming Ipswich in front of 1G45 had had to stop in front. Leaving from Platform No. 7, 1G42 had to cross the Up Main, thus blocking the progress of both southbound trains.

Entering Downham on 28 October 2022 are 387301 (rear) and 387102, with 1T14 08.42 from Kings Cross. The train has just passed the double line junction, where on 27 October 1987 several carriages of 1H18 12.35 Liverpool Street–Lynn derailed. 47576 *King's Lynn* stayed on the road.

The same morning, 387111 heads 387128 on 1T18 09.42 Kings Cross–Lynn across the Main Engine Drain, near the Downham–Littleport single line mid-point. Very poor ground means masts change sides, utilising the former Down Main bed as far as Littleport. The gentle curve is exaggerated.

It's now early afternoon as GBRf 66797 hauls 6E88 12.26 Middleton Towers–Goole Glassworks towards Ely North Junction. The Lynn and Norwich roads combine as one track, which joins the double Peterborough route and thus requires double blocking. The 'X20' sign indicates the speed limit for 'wrong road' operations over Queen Adelaide (Lynn) AHB.

Shortly after, 387106 (387119, front) on 1T30 12.42 Kings Cross–Lynn crosses that AHB. The three B1382 crossings are problematically close to each other. The EACE programme would target Adelaide, the Ely bottleneck including bridge strengthening, and many other level crossings elsewhere.

Mid-afternoon, 28 October 2022. 387112 at the rear of 1T34 13.42 Kings Cross–Lynn (387305 leading) glides towards Sandhill AHB on the southern edge of Littleport. The sun glinting on the rear lights gives the impression of an Up working!

Returning southwards later, the same pair burst into sunshine at the Cut-off Channel bridge, south of Denver TSL. Slightly reminiscent of the Denver Junction crossover once located here, the long 75 mph slue at Denver is greatly foreshortened. Six 387/3s arrived from c2c in September 2022.

November 2022, half-past midnight. Though the busy railway may be quiet it rarely sleeps. One of two units in Carriage Siding No. 1, 387305 stands by the platform used by the train cleaners, preparing for what is already 'tomorrow'. (Mark Steele)

Buildings rise at Cambridge Biomedical Campus – 20,000 jobs, expected to double within 20 years, reason for Cambridge South's proposed four twelve-car platforms. Looking northwards on 2 November 2022, 387102 and 387301 hasten towards King's Lynn with 1T34 13.42 from Kings Cross. The first GN ETCS-fitted (cab-signalling) 387 was 387101.

Great Northern's King's Lynn–Ely–Cambridge–Kings Cross trains provide the expresses. GA, Thameslink and XC operate here too. That day, 387109 is on the rear of 1T41 14.44 King's Lynn–Kings Cross, passing the site of the new station (approved 21 December 2022, target opening 2025) heading towards Nine Wells Bridge and powering on to London.